Phonics

Let's make it simple...

Foundational Phonics

Set I
Book 4

Namrata Dhawle

Made with ♥ on the Notion Press Platform
www.notionpress.com

Preface

Since the early 20th century, phonics has been widely used in primary education to teach literacy across the English-speaking world.

This syllabus is designed according to the Montessori methodology, which emphasizes guiding children through techniques that develop their awareness of sounds. Using phonics, we can effectively teach English reading and writing.

Phonics is a method for teaching reading and writing in English by fostering phonemic awareness—the ability to hear, identify, and manipulate phonemes. It establishes a connection between these sounds and the spelling patterns that represent them.

The primary goal of phonics is to enable beginning readers to decode unfamiliar written words by sounding them out or blending the sounds of spelling patterns. Since phonics focuses on spoken and written units within words, it is considered a sub-lexical approach. It is often contrasted with the whole-language philosophy, which adopts a word-level-up strategy for teaching reading.

In essence, phonics teaches reading and pronunciation through the recognition of letter sounds, letter combinations, and syllables.

To implement this learning method, teachers must begin preparing children in the nursery by raising their awareness of sounds. This involves enriching their vocabulary through exposure to small objects or pictures representing various words.

Most importantly, before starting sound games or phonics activities, it is essential to ensure that children are familiar with the words and objects being introduced.

Sincerely,
Namrata Ninad Dhawle
AMI Certified Montessori Educator
Contact:namrata.montessori@gmail.com

Guidelines for Teachers

Daily Teaching Plan :
Teachers are encouraged to be prepared with the teaching plan for the next day according to the syllabus. This will help maintain a smooth and engaging learning experience.

Workbooks Management :
Please ensure that all workbooks are kept in the classrooms to maintain organization and easy accessibility for effective learning.

Classroom Supplies :
Each classroom should be equipped with a set of **slates and chalk or blank papers and crayons** to foster creativity and interactive learning.

Group Activities :
Group activities should involve a maximum of 4-5 children per group to promote effective participation and collaboration while ensuring individual attention.

Additional Support :
Additional revision sessions should be arranged for students who may benefit from extra practice, helping them strengthen their understanding and build confidence.

Puzzle Words Preparation :
Teachers are requested to laminate and cut the provided **Puzzle Words** separately, ensuring that each classroom has one complete set of **Puzzle Words** (Set II Book 1 - Phonogram) to support literacy development.

Thank you for your dedication and commitment to creating a positive and productive learning environment.

Namrata Dhawle

Write the first sound

Write the first sound

Write the first sound

Write the first sound

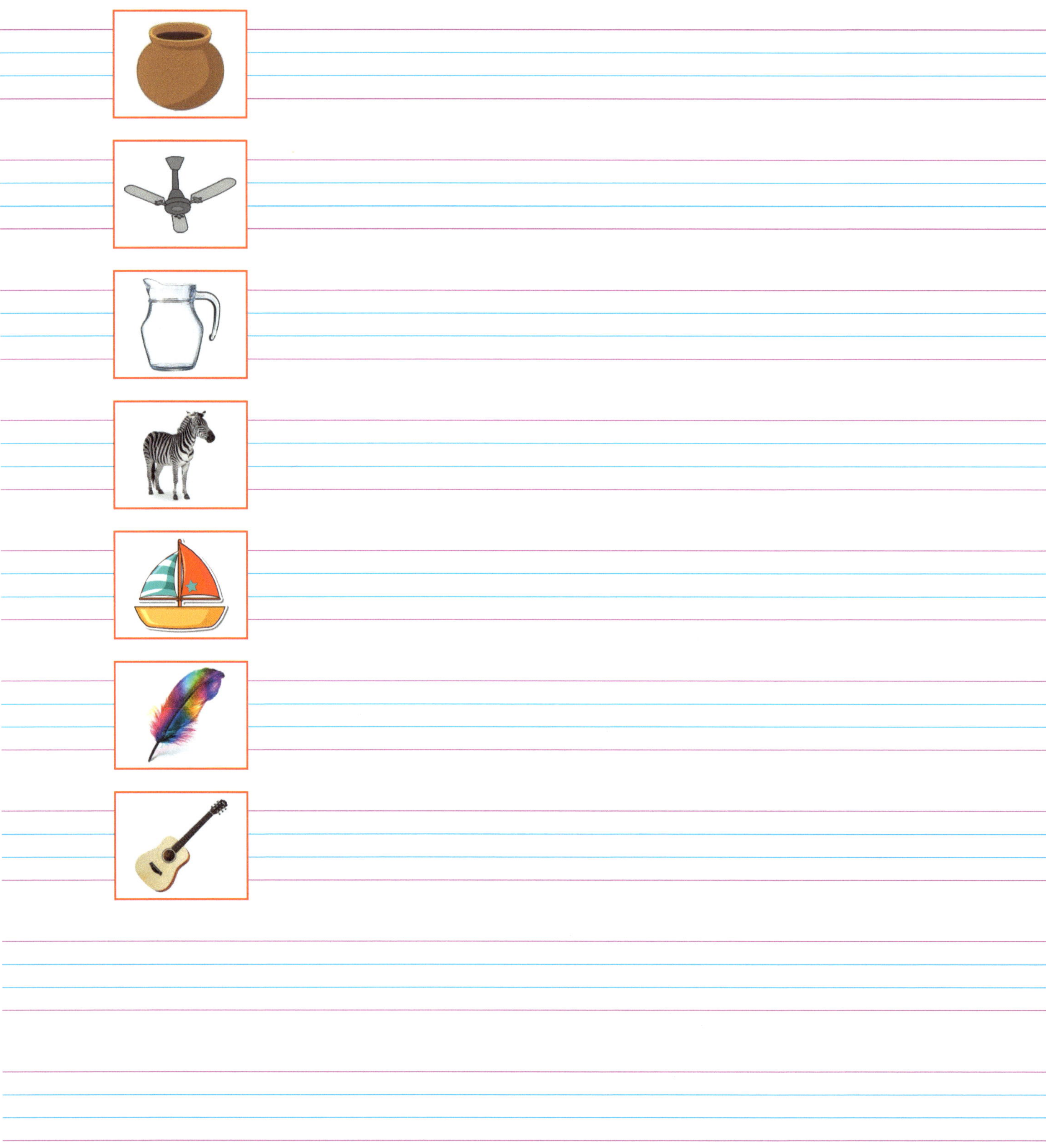

Write the first sound

_un

_ut

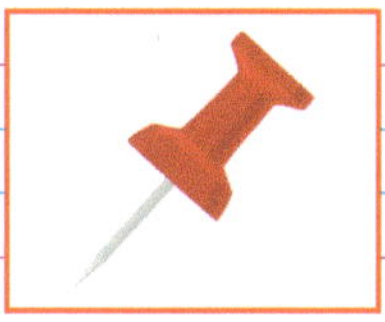

_in

_ot

_en

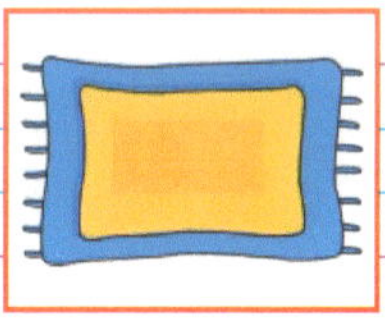

_at

_an

_ub

_og

Write the first sound

Write the first sound

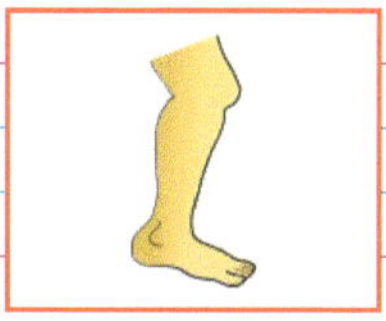

_eg

_ix

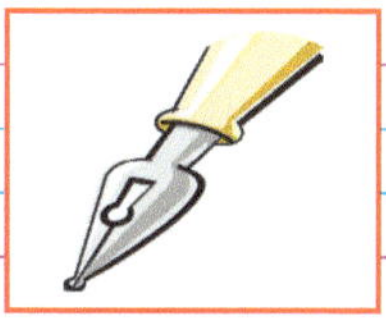

_ib

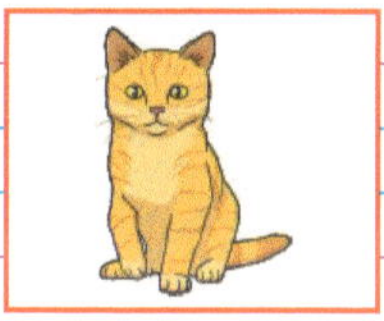

_at

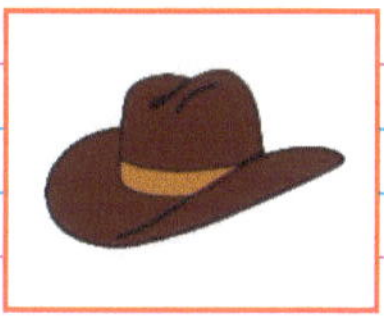

_at

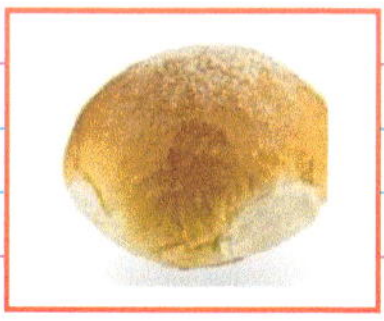

_un

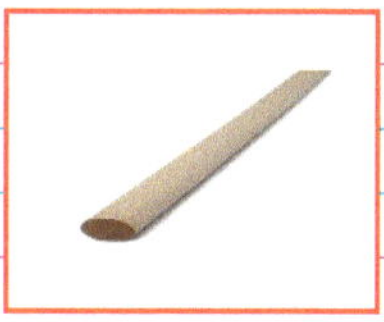

_od

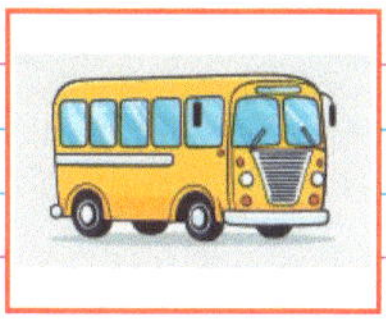

_us

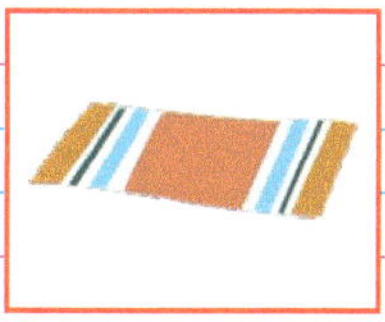

_at

Write the first sound

_an

_oy

_nt

_ag

_et

_og

_in

_ag

_ix

Write the first sound

_us

_ip

_ap

_in

_ib

_id

_ar

_un

_ox

Write the first sound

_og

_en

_en

_ot

_op

_am

_ad

_at

_nt

Write the first sound

_at

_ed

_ip

_an

_ig

_ad

_it

_un

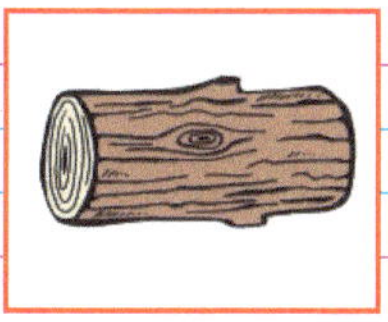

_og

Write the first sound

_ax

_eb

_ig

_ib

_in

_it

_an

_oy

_og

Write the first sound

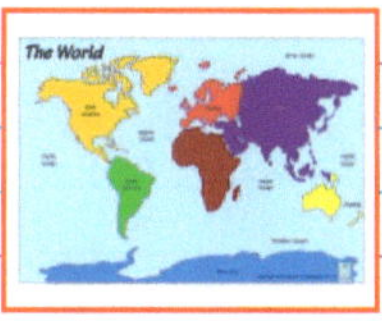

_ap

_en

_in

_ug

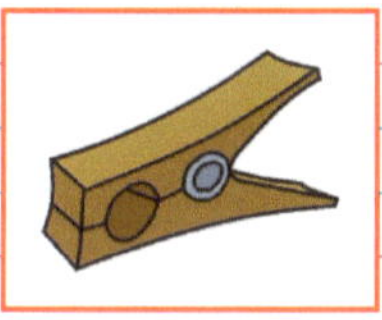

_eg

_at

_am

_an

_ig

Write the first sound

_ad

_ed

_it

_og

_ub

_am

_un

_us

_ut

Write the last sound

bu_

li_

ca_

bi_

ni_

li_

ja_

ra_

wi_

Write the last sound

do_

de_

ni_

ho_

mo

ja_

sa_

ba_

an_

Write the last sound

wa_

we_

wi_

bi_

fi _

si _

ca_

ru_

lo_

Write the last sound

ra__

be__

zi__

ma__

pi__

sa__

ra__

va__

wi__

Write the last sound

le_

si_

ni_

ca_

ha_

bu_

ro_

bu_

ma_

Write the last sound

Write the last sound

su_

hu_

pi_

po_

te_

ma_

fa_

tu_

lo_

Write the last sound

ta＿

cu＿

bo＿

ba＿

ju＿

to＿

te＿

do＿

cu＿

Write the last sound

ma __

he __

wi __

bu __

pe __

ba __

ca __

ha __

bu __

Write the last sound

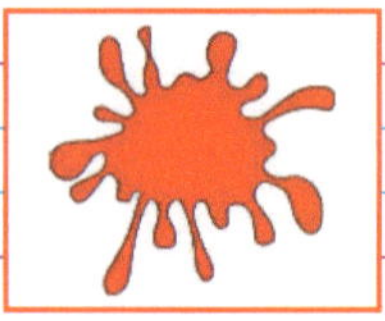

re __

ba __

he __

ho __

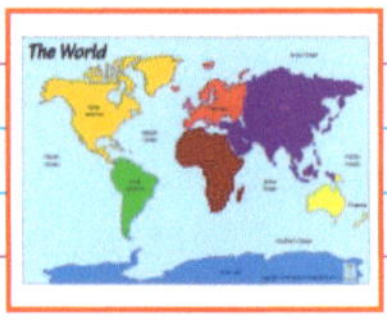

ma __

cu __

ya __

ja __

hi __

Write the middle sound

(leg)	*l__g*
6	*s__x*
(nib)	*n__b*
(cat)	*c__t*
(hat)	*h__t*
(bun)	*b__n*
(rod)	*r__d*
(bus)	*b__s*
(mat)	*m__t*

Write the middle sound

Write the middle sound

Write the middle sound

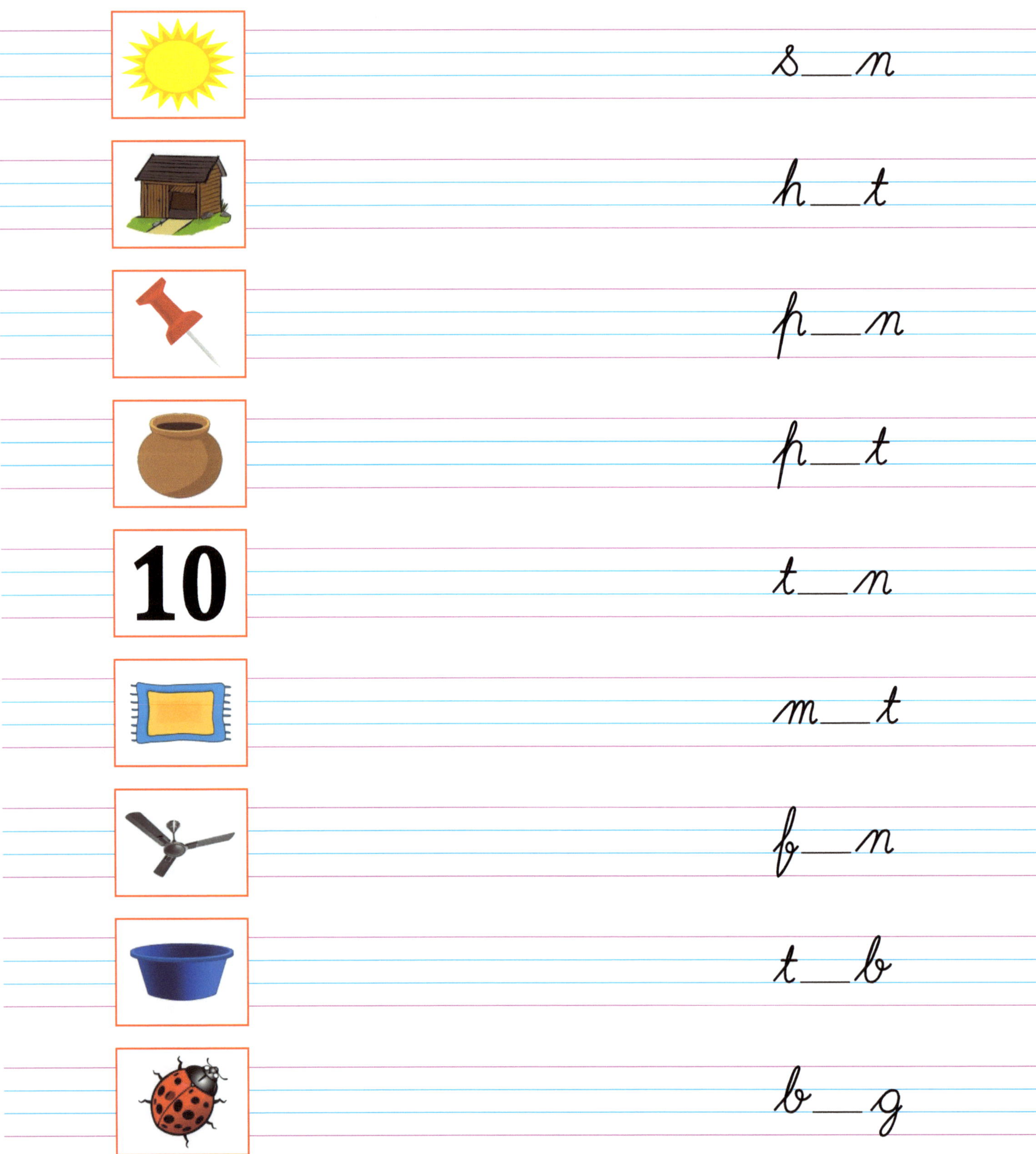

Write the middle sound

b__s

l__p

c__p

b__n

n__b

l__d

j__r

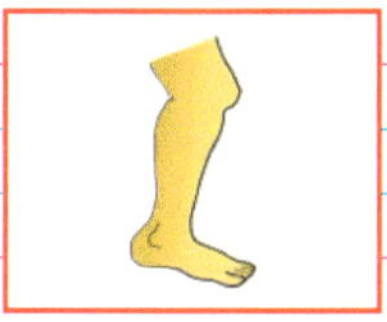

l__g

b__n

Write the middle sound

Write the middle sound

r __ t

b __ d

z __ p

m __ n

p __ g

s __ d

p __ n

n __ t

p __ n

Write the middle sound

Word
w __ x
w __ b
w __ g
b __ b
f __ n
s __ t
c __ n
c __ p
j __ g

Write the middle sound

m__p

h__n

w__n

b__g

p__g

b__t

l__p

l__d

s__n

Write the middle sound